COAST CALENDAR

Books by
ROBERT P. TRISTRAM COFFIN

POEMS
    CHRISTCHURCH
    DEW AND BRONZE
    GOLDEN FALCON
    THE YOKE OF THUNDER
    BALLADS OF SQUARE-TOED AMERICANS
    STRANGE HOLINESS
    SALTWATER FARM
    MAINE BALLADS
    COLLECTED POEMS
    THERE WILL BE BREAD AND LOVE
    PRIMER FOR AMERICA
    POEMS FOR A SON WITH WINGS
    PEOPLE BEHAVE LIKE BALLADS
    COLLECTED POEMS, NEW AND ENLARGED EDITION
    ONE-HORSE FARM
ESSAYS
    BOOK OF CROWNS AND COTTAGES
    AN ATTIC ROOM
    CHRISTMAS IN MAINE
    BOOK OF UNCLES
    MAINSTAYS OF MAINE
    YANKEE COAST
    COAST CALENDAR
BIOGRAPHIES
    LAUD: STORM CENTER OF STUART ENGLAND
    THE DUKES OF BUCKINGHAM
    PORTRAIT OF AN AMERICAN (*The Author's Father*)
    CAPTAIN ABBY AND CAPTAIN JOHN (*Abby and John Pennell,*
       Brunswick, Maine)
AUTOBIOGRAPHY
    LOST PARADISE (*The Author's Life to His Twelfth Year*)
NOVELS
    RED SKY IN THE MORNING
    JOHN DAWN
    THOMAS-THOMAS-ANCIL-THOMAS
LECTURES
    NEW POETRY OF NEW ENGLAND (*Frost and Robinson*)
       (*The Turnbull Memorial Lectures,* Johns Hopkins University)
    THE SUBSTANCE THAT IS POETRY
       (*The Patten Lectures,* Indiana University)
    THE THIRD HUNGER & THE POEM ALOUD
       (*The Samuel Harris Lectures,* Bangor Theological Seminary)
       (*Speech Club Lecture,* Texas State College for Women)
HISTORY
    KENNEBEC: CRADLE OF AMERICANS
       (*The Rivers of America Series*)
TEXTS
    A BOOK OF SEVENTEENTH-CENTURY PROSE
    SEVENTEENTH-CENTURY PROSE AND POETRY
       (*Both with A. M. Witherspoon*)

COAST CALENDAR

ROBERT P. TRISTRAM COFFIN

Decorations by the Author

Down East Books
Camden, Maine

ISBN: 0-89272-632-6

Printed and bound by Versa Press, Inc., East Peoria, Illinois.

2   3   1

Down East Books
Camden, Maine
Book orders: 800-685-7962
www.downeastbooks.com
A division of Down East Enterprise,
publishers of *Down East* magazine
www.downeast.com

Originally published in 1947 by the Bobbs-Merrill Company, Inc.

Library of Congress Control Number: 2003108985

To

LEDLIE AND PRISCILLA

WHO FOLLOW THE CALENDAR THROUGH

ON A MAINE FARM

AND WHO HAVE FOLLOWED MY BOOKS AND ME

THROUGH MANY GOLDEN MAINE YEARS

And

To

ALL THE LITTLE BERRYS

MY GODDAUGHTER DIANA

DAVID

BRUCE

Grateful acknowledgment is made by the author to *Gourmet Magazine,* in whose pages some of his text and some of his pictures first appeared, and to Arthur L. Guptill, another down-Maine man, who helped to design this book about the state.

COAST CALENDAR

★ ★ ★ *January* ★ ★ ★

COMES IN THE NEW YEAR AND GALES. Now the world whitens with strong blizzards. The winds fall, the sun is too bright to look at, and the shadows of the straight white birch lie blue and curved along the domed drifts. The outer islands show like cubes of sugar on the blue-black of the bold Atlantic. But the upper bays are white, and the corded wood comes home from the islands on sleds. The horses' breaths float like plumes on each side. Now the old man hugs the stove, but the small boy's seat is brave with parti-colored patches from his brother and his father; he goes ramping down the hill on his sled and kicks up diamonds with his glad toes. The big boy will have no part of sliding but sandpapers the oars to his boat like a man.

The only birds are the splinters of diamond-and-jet which cry *chick-a-dee-dee*, sharp as needles among the pines. The Arctic owl is inquiring for mice at midnight. The wife heats the corn and runs to the henhouse with the hot pan in her apron. The fox leaves a line of dimples as he trots through the snowy woods, the mice leave a featherstitching, and the cuneiforms around the dead stump tell where the ruffed partridge has been to his dinner. The only berries are the red rose hips, and the crinkle-tipped boxberries hang over the jet trickle of water below the arch of snow. The winds have an edge like a whet knife, and a sad song hangs around the chimney. It gets darker later each evening.

As the days grow longer
The cold grows stronger.

The thermometer falls below zero, the high moon blazes like noon, and the lonesome white bays crack for pain of the cold. Honey-bees crawl to new combs and warm themselves in the hive at the heat of last summer's sun. The stars snap like sapphires, you hear the hiss of their burning, and the teapot hisses continuously on the back of the stove. The barrel of quahaugs in the cellar is halfway down.

The January thaw comes, it slushes up and rains. For a spider has crawled out of his corner, as the old man notes, and it has moderated suddenly, with the mercury climbing red in the glass. The small boy's nose is as scarlet as rose hips as he snuffles with his feet in hot water and mustard by the fire. *Aquarius* is the sign, and he turns out a blue-flowered, five-gallon jug on every last hillside.

The world hardens up in a night and turns to pure glass. The only flowers are the icicles on the eaves and the beads on each twig. The sun jumps out of the Atlantic, a man goes out into a world that is a single cut diamond. Forests and mountains are too bright to look at with wide-open eyes. The night blazes with thousands of stars tangled into every tree. The only fish now are the silver shavings of smelts. It blossoms small white houses up and down the hard, white creeks, and big men crouch over little lanterns burning at noonday and pull up the smelts through the hole in the floor.

The pine needles hug together, and the dark color of them, the old man says, foretells a coming storm. The woodchuck sleeps in his burrow, with never a whimper, and the hound dog bays the white-circled moon. Grandpa sees three stars inside the moon's circle, so the storm is three days away. Sure enough, the stars were right; a great fall of snow buries the bays and houses on the third day. The farmer oils up his harnesses. He shovels a canyon to the boathouse for a single hammer he needs.

Now the toolshed hums. The father works with smoking breath on the oak keel of his new boat, and the bright-eyed small boy watches and holds things with shavings in his yellow hair. No such bright days and nights ever as now. The earth runs emerald and gold and silver, for now the year is afire with January, and life is tip-a-toe. The cows stand all day in golden straw, and their breath smokes up the tie-up. The little girls cut out strings of paper dolls with joined hands. A haymow is a joy to smell on a cold afternoon. The small boy lies by his boy-friend and whispers tremendous secrets in the hay. The farmer's wife runs up a mince pie and marks a flock of spring geese across it with a silver knife and slips it into the oven.

An old book is a good dish for a long night. Grandfather thumbs the *Old Farmer's Almanac* as he sits on the woodbox back of the stove. There will be plenty more snow. The little dog lies under the cookstove and bakes himself through like a biscuit. The young boy smells the newsprint of the *Boston Transcript* around the hot brick that warms his toes in bed. It snows two feet. The farmer knits a lobster-head as he sits with his stocking feet in the oven, which still smells of mince pie. The keel is finished in the toolshed. It snows three feet. Grandmother's needles fly, and a mountain of socks is rising by her Boston rocker. The young man breaks the axe-helve by striking over the beech chopping-block, but it is because his mind is full of a tall girl with tight braids. The big boy tries chewing-tobacco when Grandpa is not looking to his plug. It tastes bad, but it is strong man-food.

Cows are led smoking to the watering tubs by the well, and the dog lifts his leg and leaves an orange lace on the snow. The small boy writes his small name in the same orange lace beside his father's heavy signature on the white wall of the path. Nights, the men catch up with the news with the unaccustomed spectacles on the ends of their noses. The new snowstorm roars through the spruces, and the flakes go up as much as down. The winds are north or northwest ones, and they rattle old teeth and old hemlocks.

The dish of the month is pork gravy. The wife of the house gets a chunk of salt pork from the barrel down-cellar and cuts it into pieces the size of her husband's thumb. She fries the pieces in the spider till they are an airy brown and are ready to float out of the seething fat. She mixes her flour thickening, a pint of water, and two tablespoons of flour already stirred into two tablespoons of water and all the lumps gotten out. She douses in the pint of thickening into the smoking spider, the fire at white heat from the birch-wood, and she stirs it into a creamy miracle with her iron spoon. She stirs and stirs and uses only her foot to drive the cat away from the codfish she is preparing to go with the gravy. The gravy boils right up and down and thickens around the flying spoon. Mother takes it off at its peak and pours it into the yellow bowl. She sets it at the heart of the table, with the ladling spoon ready. It is for the codfish today. But it is for roast beef tomorrow, for potatoes white or yellow, for all the meats, and for all the fish. It is the backbone of winter's feasting. It is the Rock of Gibraltar of Maine.

It snows, it snows.

The hired man keeps close to the barn. The long icicles on his moustache make him look like a walrus as he shovels out the bonfires the cows have left on the tie-up floor and sprinkles new chaff under the cows. The crows crowd together in the deep spruce thickets, but there is no heat in their shrunken bones, and they find nothing to say.

The small boy steals away to go sliding with the small girl with molasses-candy curls and five freckles across her tipped-up nose. He never lets her feet touch the ground. He pulls her back up every hill on his sled, digging in his toes. Every view the girl has, the seat of the boy's second-best corduroy breeches is the center of all. The window-panes of the woodshed are forests of white palm trees, and the small boy has to breathe a long time to get a hole in the glass big enough to peek through with one blue eye. The hired man takes the heifers to the watering tub, and a playful young lady in velvet takes a turn around his pants leg with her rope and turns him broadside up in the snow.

Grandpa crowds the wood into the kitchen stove, and the woodbox goes down a foot an hour. The small boy totters from the shed under armful after armful of beech and birch, and his breath goes blue before him on the air. Grandpa spreads his long legs wide to the stove grate and sops up all the heat there. The hired man spreads his wide seat to the other whole side of the stove, and it is a very narrow boy that can get close enough to the stove to get any good from it. The scream of the bucksaw goes on hour by hour in the shed, the big boy fills the floor with sawdust and new sticks for the small boy to tier up. Grandpa toasts some cheese over the open stove and gives some to the small boy. The girls litter the floor with dolls and doll-clothes so there is no place for a man's big feet. Grandma tries to mend a doll's broken head, but the hired man upsets the glue-pot, and the doll goes to bed without her hair.

The snow is on every window sash. More is coming thick on the air.

It is a long month, a hard month, the fish and the furrows take a good rest, and a boat is being born. The January world is a world as much inside as out, and a good one. *Selah!*

COAST CALENDAR

★ ★ ★ February ★ ★ ★

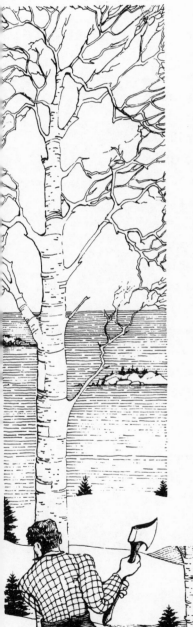

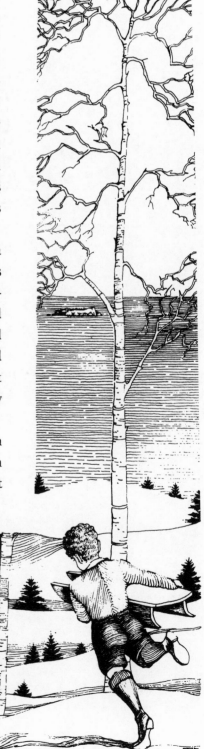

COMES IN A SPELL OF WEATHER, SNOW-squalls, sleet, rain, and snow. But Candlemas Day dawns clear, and John Henry Woodchuck sticks out his snout, sees his shadow, and jumps back abed for another six weeks' snooze. The reach boat in the shed grows, the oak backbone sprouts oak ribs, and the star-eyed boy holds against his father as the man drives home the blue bolts in the fragrant red wood. Now is a great business of boring the maples and hanging the sap-pails in the long-shadowed woods. The axe rings on the beech, the echo answers it under the hill, and the cordwood piles up between the fir stakes. Brush fires turn an afternoon warm, and the azure smoke makes the red squirrel cough as he scolds, turning the fir-cone in his expert hands and picking out the winged seeds. The boy burns holes in his breeches his mother will scold much to mend.

The hired man consumes nearly his weight in cut-plug a week, and he borrows from Grandpa's box when no one is looking. The little yellow dog runs rabbits among the balsams all the short day, his nose is hot on their three-lobed tracks. The rabbits take him through every briar bush and juniper. He comes home beat out and lies under the stove and chases rabbits in his dreams. The crows are down to the last misshapen kernels in the corn ears of the upper garden. They roost for days without moving a feather.

The apples are three-quarters gone in the cellar. The barn cat is as fat as a porpoise because of the fat mice in the grain bin. The great Arctic owl on his popple stump booms out at midnight with a question nobody answers, and the sleek wood mice tremble to their toes. The deer paw for the grass kept green by the running water. It is the month of pinched bellies.

Grandpa comes down with a cold from sitting tarring twine in the shed and gets a mustard plaster to his chest for his sins. The hired man misses two rabbits ahead of the yellow dog, but the big boy knocks three bunnies over. The hired man eats more rabbit dumplings than he should and groans in his open-chamber room the livelong night. A widow also is on his mind.

The bees have heat enough in their hives, for they work their glassy wings and make heat out of their golden selves. The grandpa of all the rabbits does not come home, and the Arctic owl, plump as his stump, knows more than he should but says nothing. Grandpa is up from his plaster but comes down with a crick in his back and gets another plaster there. Grandma starts her third crazy quilt. It turns moderate and thaws, it drizzles rain, comes off cold and freezes. The partridge by the boiling spring finds himself tombed up in ice, and his pecking grows weaker as the days pass. Bright death stares him in the face.

The hired man cheats at parcheesi, but the small boy beats him all hollow in spite of it. Nighttimes, the kitchen smokes with the mittens and socks of the woodcutters. The small boy turns the woodshed grindstone for his father's axe until his hands are two blisters. Mother runs up a yard of johnnycake for supper. The girls get their feet soaked sliding, and they go to bed goose-greased. Grandpa reads the *Family Doctor* till he believes he is on the edge of consumption, but Grandma mixes up mustard for a new plaster. Mother steams the pieces of oak in her teakettle and runs with them hot to Father, and Father bends them into place in the curving sides of his boat.

It comes off a sudden thaw, the starving partridge emerges from the icy crust and beats his wings till he reaches the rose hips and eats till his strength returns. The Arctic owl has located his supper, but when he sails noiselessly down among the new snowflakes, he finds only a few draggled feathers under the briar bush. He returns to his perch and waits for a belated rabbit. But the rabbits are early to bed, and the owl goes empty all night and troubles the woods with his queries. It snows twelve inches. It is hungry weather.

Now the hearth glows late into the night, and Father sits with the small girl on one knee and the small boy on the other and sings and tells stories. The corncobs of the hired man and Grandpa make a blue fog of the room. Mother runs up a pair of wool stockings. Grandma dozes with her steel-rimmed glasses on the end of her nose, and her old skin looks like the apple blossoms of May as she leans towards the firelight. The big boy comes from the cellar covered with cobwebs and turns out the amber cider into glasses from his blue-flowered jug. The hired man dips his big moustache deep in his mug and dreams of a widow. The small boy sips from his father's glass, and falls off asleep.

Russets and Baldwins are low in the bin, but the strings of dried apples from the open-chamber bring back the taste of summer in a hot pie. The manure pile steams in the sun by the barn. Evenings, the kernels in the wire box over the open stove-cover explode into hot snowballs, the woman of the house pours on molasses and melted butter, and makes the balls which will keep the mouths of boys and girls busy till bedtime. The school children read about log cabins and Lincoln. The farmer cuts transparent chunks from the folios of salted hake and eats them with his hot meal porridge. Now the scissors flash, and the girls, with their tongues following the curving of the scissors, turn out lattices of hearts from white and red paper; the little boy goes with his heart in his mouth and pushes his misspelled missive, garnished with a vast beef heart, under the door of the small girl with molasses-candy curls. He has written for keeps.

> *Sweethart I am thyne*
> *Wunt you be my Vallantine.*

The ocean chafes out beyond the white ice, and the long, white fires of its spray burn along the horizon. The yoked oxen drag the pine logs for next year's dory from the swamp, and there is much yelling of *whoa-hish! gee-haw!* and using of the goad on the off-ox. The big boy sharpens the axe and spits out of the corner of his mouth like a man; he leaves a yellow star on the snow. Two feet of snow fall. The bees keep the hive warm with their winnowing wings. The Father of our Country is wreathed in red-white-and-blue crêpe paper in the steel engraving on the east wall of the school. A freckled boy with beanpot handles for ears says farewell to his officers and brothers in Cincinnati who have founded a nation out of shopkeepers, plowmen, and lawyers. It snows. It snows. It snows.

The rabbit in the swamp eats the top buds off the alders. Grandma sees the new moon over her left shoulder and trembles. She breaks the steel bows on her spectacles next day. The whitening buds on the waxy arbutus are four feet under the white level of the world. The only fresh fish are small smelts, but the women piecen them out with red Kennebec turkeys from the long sticks in the smokehouse; they pinch the herrings' tails under the stove-cover, let them hang down to the coals, pull them out all ablaze; and the smell of herring scents up the whole house. The men fall to with watering mouths and eat their fiery supper.

Pisces is the sign, and though the fresh cod are idling deep in Atlantic, salt cod with pork gravy saffrons the noon.

The lantern lights the tie-up windows in the dead of the night, and there is a wobbly-legged calf for the young boy to hug in the morning. All the girls get new dresses, and the sewing machine sings beyond the rising of the evening star. The boys get new breeches cut out of Father's pants. The young man slicks down his hair for the Grange Sociable, he bids for the basket of the girl with tight braids, and eats her pound-cake with her, his heart beating fast and his head as light as a feather.

Now men look to their lobster traps in the fishhouse, the wormed laths are replaced with new, and the triple bows of spruce are renailed. The winds box the compass. But the strongest and longest are swinging more towards the south. Grandpa sits on the *Youth's Companion* to keep it from the small boy. The hens cackle loud with reddened combs in the melting snow at noon, the rooster treads on his wing to them, he struts on only the tips of his toes, barely touching the ground. The baskets come heaping full of warm eggs now, when the sun slips down behind the western pines and the snow hardens to ivory.

The dish of the month is halibuts' heads. The small boy brings three of the wide-mouthed heads from the frosty barrel in the shed. The women gouge out the eyes and soak the heads in warm water and scrape them. They put them into the greased bake-pan and lace with powdered herbs and ribbons of salt pork; they pop them into the oven, with a red-oak-wood fire going full blast, and sit back and relax and let the odors of the delectable compromise of fat and lean meat in the halibuts' heads fill the kitchen, fill the house, fill the woods beyond. And the men and boys come running home to dinner and crunch the crisp, brown, crackling meat, and even the bones, to get the last goodness out of the good deep-sea flesh. And they eat so much that they cannot return to the wood-chopping.

It is a cold month, a snowy month, and the ocean is locked up tight. But days are lengthening out, the sap is flowing up in men and maples. The world is a promise of growing.

COAST CALENDAR

⋆ ⋆ ⋆ *March* ⋆ ⋆ ⋆

COMES IN WITH VAST WINDS. THE OAKS roar loud on the bay, the elms sing high over the house all the night, the sun rolls out of the ocean like a golden ox-cart wheel, and March comes in like the Lion. A blizzard twilights the noon, but the clouds rip apart, and the arms of the climbing young sun come down with long light and handle the blinding jewels of the ice-bound islands on the sea.

The dish of the month is pigs' feet with dumplings. The women bring in the pig-trotters stiff with winter from the woodshed, they wash them well, sousing them in cold water to get out the frost. Then they cook them over a slow fire in the big iron kettle, till the feet grow tender, and they salt them to taste. When the meat is ready to fall from the bones, they throw into the kettle sliced onions and a clove of garlic. While these are seething, the womenfolks run up the dumplings, taking two cups of sifted flour and a teaspoon of salt and pouring in water till the dough can be rolled out flat on the breadboard with the rolling-pin. They cut the cloth of dough into rectangles that shrink away from the knife, douse the rectangles into the soup one by one, and keep them apart as they cook for fifteen minutes. Or if there is extra hard work for the menfolks outside, the women make dough-devils, instead of dumplings, and fill the pot to the cover with the exploding snowballs of flour.

Men watch the line of dark blue beyond the headlands like so many fish hawks. It is wider this morning than it was last evening. The wind shakes the pinewoods into a high dust of ground diamonds. The lobster traps pile up like ribbed martyrs in the snow. Nights are bleatings of new lambs, and under clouds of stars a man brings into lamplight a weak thing with a thin cry. The little girls waken and see the new woolen baby nursing at the bottle on the hearth. They baby him in their arms, and he runs about the house on legs much too large for him.

The reach boat has grown up over the windows in the toolshed, and the man talks to the boy through a wall of curved pine. Ledges towards the sun are showing like ribs, pussywillows star the twilight. The hen-house shakes with song, it rains eggs, and the roosters are in full cry with bronze, bristling necks. The price of eggs goes to the bottom, the wife's pitcher gets no new silver, and the men get eggs morning and noon and night. The snow of the yard smokes with hen-droppings. The world rises two white feet in a night, and the big boy carries the small boy pig-a-back through the drifts.

Aries has his head down and butts against the world, and his fleece tufts with white every fence and stone wall. The young man walks ten snowy miles to say ten words to a girl three islands away. He risks his life on thinned ice, but counts it worth the risk. A snowdrift goes down a foot under one day of the sun. The hams are getting down to the small ends, and the smokehouse is empty racks and rafters. But there is a smell of ocean and the south in the air. The boys and girls go to school over the bay ice but carry their long poles by the middles now in case the footing should give way.

Winds are out of the north, out of the east, then out of the south; the vane is wearing loose on its ferrule. The cows are restless at their stanchions; the mows are low enough for a boy to leap off them, the hay is half chaff. The big boy goes into long pants and begins to walk like his father. The children toe the mark and line up for their sulphur-and-molasses. The mother makes camphor bags for their necks against colds. It snows, it blows, it rains; it sleets, it blows, it snows again. It is clear as crystal, and a thousand summer clouds run by without getting in the sun's way. Days are like diamonds.

A mother hen sits on a checkerboard of sunlight in the shed, and twenty-two new eyes as bright as blueberries gaze out from under the feathers on her widened wings. The broom falls across the door, and the old man swears it means a stranger is coming. It turns out true. The old cradle has a new tenant, and his eyes are flakes of the sudden blue between March clouds.

> *A son that's born in shiny March*
> *Is full of iron, stars, and starch.*

The winds blow up into a peak and a gale. The house trembles. The sun has leapt the Line and is headed north up the curve of the globe. The bay booms the night long. At sunrise, all the white bays are dark blue water full of white swans of ice cakes. The backbone of winter is broken, the larder is unlocked! Old men and young men are wading the snowdrifts in a race for young clams. They turn over the ice cakes and dredge up the grooved quahaugs. The family eat them raw and dripping from the shell. Supper is tender clams fried in batter, and the house is like a tree full of bluebirds in full throat.

Spring is here with both feet, in two feet of snow. The children go to school by boat now, though the ways are still icy. The high-run tides of the year fill every cove and almost float away the fishhouse. Arrowhead after arrowhead of wild geese goes north, the birds' heads float free ahead of their long necks, and the sound of their honking goes endlessly over through the night. The boat in the toolshed is all decked in forward. Now an old uncle brings on his horse-sled the first skiff for a new boy-sailor in short pants. The boy sits in it in the yard and rows with dry oars, the whole Pacific is in his blue eyes. Mother hears the first robin, and she flies to her scrub-pail and white paint, the house smells like peppermint and shines like a scoured pan.

The woodchuck climbs from his hole, he sits brown in the sun, wrinkling up his nose to the smell of growing roots. New wallpaper goes on, the girls wash their hair and lean over with it hanging in the sun. The cows are down to the bottom of the bin of middlings. Drifts disappear in a day. Green snakes of water dart through the quagmires of the roads. The earth is full of blue holes with sky in them, and the ducks make merry with quacking the livelong day. Fleets of their feathers sail on the pools. The fishhouse hums with saws and hammers, brush is lifted from the dories. And the end of the toolshed swings open, and two yoke of oxen drag the high-nosed reach boat to the cove, with the small boy in it floating on air. The good smell of paint is blown along the wind, the boat turns white outside and green in; the engine is blocked up in place and the shaft and propeller lined up true. The huge boat rides the rollers and goes into the sea. All the dories slide into the water. The young boy's boat takes her maiden dip.

The boys stand at the bows of their skiffs with raised darts and watch for the bulges of flounders' eyes on the sun-shot mud. The first flounder of the year fries and fills the house with hunger. Now the brown pasture burns with a dozen tall fires, the sons drag the cut junipers starred with emerald stones, and the father burns them on the ledge. Under a sky spilling windy stars, the small boy sleeps rolled up in the blanket with his father, and they keep warm all night from the heat in the ledge where they burned the junipers. The Indians' soapstone, the father calls this warm bed of rock, it has been handed on down to him from the ancient Abenakis. It is a red-letter night in a boy's life.

Diapers flap from the back doorstep to the shed's end, clothespins let go in the gale, and diapers lie like patches of snow among the spruces.

Next to the lingering snowdrift, under the hot dead leaves, the small boy smells out the first Mayflowers. He uncovers a score of pink and white stars. He goes with skipping heart and leaves them, hot with the heat of his hand, in a bunch at the door of the little girl who one day will bear him his fair-haired sons. The big boy snorts at girls and makes him a clam-rocker out of his father's laths, when his father is not looking. But the boy in a man's pants picks a bunch of Mayflowers, when no one is watching, and he lays the blossoms down with his heart at the feet of the island girl. She takes up both with deep blushes.

The small yellow dog runs up and down all the greening hills, and the new ram lambs live more on sky than on earth, they leap up so often. The crows come swarming back to life and fill the world with cawing. Grandma takes her first spring air on the side porch, wrapped deep in her shawl. The hired man combs out his moustache wide at the sink, washes behind his ears for the first time in months, and goes off stepping high in his best pants towards the widow two farms away. The hives suddenly boil over with bees, and golden bullets go off to what May-flowers the boys and love have left on the hillside. Grandpa whittles the small boy a small schooner in the sun. The partridge spreads his bronze ruff to the sun. He begins to think of love and drumming.

The winds fall, the nights turn mild. And March goes out like a woolly ewe-lamb.

COAST CALENDAR

★ ★ ★ *April* ★ ★ ★

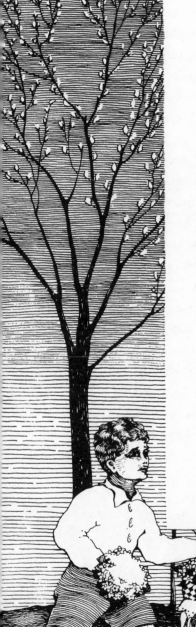

BEGINS WITH MAY AIRS. THE ADDER casts his skin and leaves it like a curl of spring sky on the hot ledge; and the farmer sloughs off his thick flannels. But the old man feels the cold still in his narrow bones, and he sticks to his long-ones. The south slopes of the hills scent the south winds with Mayflowers. The first few flies bumble about in the kitchen. It turns sharp in a night, and the ducks waddle sad on a hard and waterless world. Grandma dreams of white roses, and there will be a death in the family within the year. The sun comes out hot. Brooks run like wildfire. Catkins shake out their gilt tassels on the popple trees. Comes a freeze, and the loud little brooks fall quiet. It snows deep. The sun comes out strong. All the snow melts. The ducks are wild on many sudden waters.

The cosset lamb grows into a burden and is turned out of the kitchen to fend for himself where the green blades of grass are pricking through the world.

It rains, and it clears. It rains, and it shines.

The feast of the season is alewives. For the fattest of the herring have returned, and the land near all the brooks is frosted with their scales. The Abenaki fish steams in all kitchens, and the rich aroma of it baking and roasting and frying and broiling and boiling and sousing in vinegar goes out over the whole coast. The woman of the house fries it in butter, and the man and the children let it melt in their mouths and blow out the myriads of bones. The woman boils it with pork, and the family pushes out the lacework of bones on their tongues. The woman bakes it in the family beanpot, with vinegar added and strips of salt pork, cloves, and cinnamon, and there are no bones to blow out at all.

Frog spawns string miles of jet-and-crystal beads through the marsh pond. The small boy is up to his busy butts in watery business, and his new rubber boots come home full of water. He gets it laid on to his breeches in the woodshed for his third wet feet in a morning; and the heat of his father's broad hand wards off the fever and snuffles. The horse sled is greased and put up, the crosscut saw is oiled and hung on the rafter. The children are greased deep with goose grease, and it will be a sharp cold that will get through it. In the swamp the tree stumps bleed a honey that attracts the gilt flies. Now the farmer looks to his plow, his whiffletrees and his axles, there is great mending of cart wheels and jingling of chains and harness; gear is made ready against the minute the frost is all out of the ground.

Sudden, one clear twilight, under the first dewdrop star, the peepers begin, their silvery notes spread out thick as the stars are over the meadows. Ways grow foul, carts go hub-deep in yellow mud. A fortnight passes with no getting to town. The woman of the house scrapes the bottom of the flour barrel, but she cuts her coat to suit her cloth and makes out with a big pan of johnnycake. And there is hot lobster stew, pink with coral, for supper. The big boy digs his three bushels of clams a tide and puts his silver coins in the stocking towards the new twenty-two rifle.

A wild gander goes over the waves with a taut neck stretched towards Labrador, and the high-nosed reach boat falls quickly behind him. The hired man sleeps late in a dream of his widow. The yellow dog sheds his hair, and he is a burden to the housekeeper. The crows meet in vast conclave at the ebb of the tide and gorge themselves on young crabs and broken clams the diggers have left till their crops are so large they can scarcely waddle. Partridges grow fat on the birch buds. The bees eat the last of last year's honey.

Grandpa sits in the skiff in the sun, fishing for flounders and dreaming of his long-ago boyhood. Grandma in her Boston rocker follows the sun along the boards in the kitchen floor, but she wears her shawl still on her narrow shoulders. Winter lingers in old bones.

The earliest bluets whiten the hill under the beeches, and the first dogtooth violets cover the valleys with leaves like spotted snakes. The robins come in from the South and begin pairing. The redbreasted couples look over the old nests with an eye to repairs. The bluebirds fall like flakes of sky upon the red maples. The skunk cabbage unrolls scarlet in the swamp, and the bees come to pay their first call. The woodpecker fills all the woods and the world with his hollow knocking. There is much rubbing of noses and playing of tag among the rabbits. The children play tag late till the stars are hung on the birches. The hired man washes his ears and goes towards his widow.

Now the bay blossoms with white-and-green buoys, the new lobster boat is busy, and the man of the farm comes home laden with dark green dragons. The small boy stands by his father and heads out to sea, the spray from the bone in her mouth snows them over and over. The sea-gulls have come down from inland, they follow the boat and the bait, they cry high for joy of the sea and spring. The girls are papering the playhouse. White herring are climbing the falls of the stream to lay their eggs in sweet water. The men dip them by barrels. The smoke-house starts smoking. Mother beats the rugs on the clothesline to storms of dust between squalls of snow and quick rain. There are dirty patches of snow in the sprucewoods still, but green grass is pricking the south-sloping sides of ditches.

The breeches on the small boy are a sight for each evening, for he sops up the black mud and the blue on his base of operations. The girls bake a batch of mud pies in the sun. The woodchuck is full of tender sprouts, and he meditates an addition to his family and a new sitting-room. The children cough and sneeze, and the jar of goose grease comes out again. The young boy is as slippery with it as the eel he has caught is with the gurry. The hylas and frogs sing faster and faster, and the long evenings are like a thousand sleigh bells.

Taurus now is the sign, the little ram lambs leap up with stiff legs five feet into the sky, they jump over their mother and race six together the length of the meadow. The young man blushes to think what he thinks when the girl of the island fills his mind. The days are quicksilver, the evenings clear amber. Fresh food comes dripping from the flats and the fathoms. People eat well and live high. The farmer goes early to bed to his woman. The small boy makes the small girl with the molasses curls a willow whistle on the long way from school, slipping the bark off with spit and notching the slot. He blows notes on it till the girl's eyes swim with adoration, she drinks in his wide-eared beauty under swollen buds, which look like so many silver buttons as they run with the fire of the new moon. She aches. He aches all over.

> *Love in April is like a silver knife,*
> *Kiss a girl in April, kiss her for life.*

The bluebirds are back, the robins are back; the yellowhammers, the song sparrows come in with a rush at sunup; birds fill the woods up with rolling bubbles of music.

The tall boy in man's clothes is turning the old shack at the cove into a neat cottage, and his eyes are as bright as the new ten-penny nails he is driving into his rising home. The wicker eel pots turn out yellow-bellied eels, and the small boy, empty for love, eats the chevroned brown fried eels till he founders. Grandma has her eels smothered. The cows are let out hungry to the new grass; they ride one another's backs, and the bull will have much business among them. The young man blushes like a beet to see them. The bees crawl out of the hive and turn to golden bullets, but except for a few drops of honey from the last Mayflowers, they come scolding home empty.

Now they take away the brush from the house, and lay bare the ice under. New brush fires send up zigzagging stars. The big boy and his father get their dip nets and go through the dusk to the surging brook with a lantern. The small boy tags adhesively along. The arrows of smelts come up over the rocks, then men dip them out of the air and the pools, the small boy takes off his cap and fills it with live slivers of silver. They fry the fish by the water's edge, and eat them with scraps of salt pork in an ecstasy under an arch of stars.

Ponds break up now, and the trout rises to the slender green flies. The new baby smiles his first smile, and the whole family are proud to see it. The girls make many paper baskets and hang them deep with pink, green, blue, and yellow curls of tissue, twisting it up into long curls like their own with a flick of the blade of the scissors. The small boy goes trailing clouds of tissue streamers to Molasses-Curls' house. His heart pounds louder than the knocker on the door, he drops the May basket, gumdrops and all, and he runs for dear life. But the small girl catches him at the stone wall's angle, and the boy gets his first kiss away from home. He comes home in taut breeches, treading right on the twinkling stars. He swells like the buds.

It is a month of buds and little boys in love, and of great promises, for all its mud and snow, and life moves out of the house at last and under the good sun.

COAST CALENDAR

★ ∴ ★ ★ *May* ★ ★ ∵ ★

COMES IN WEST WINDS AND A SKY
snowing lambs. The empty barn echoes, but the bay bobs
with boats. Grandma's rocker and Grandma are put out on
the south side porch. The world greens in a night, and the
cows keep their sweet mouths to the ground all day long.
There are snowdrifts in deep dingles and among thick
spruces, but there are bluets frosting all other ground. Pussy-
paws rise in the pasture, and the mullein pushes out woolen
new leaves. The heron arrives from Florida and walks the
cove by golden moonlight, thoughtfully, as becomes a much-
traveled person. Mummie-chubs crowd the pools, and the
small boy smells to high heaven of fish in all his breeches'
pockets. Marbles and hoops roll out on the earth now. But the
big boy has put such childish things away. He gives his young
brother his best glass alley, and goes in his boat after cunners.

Grandpa hears the first cuckoo and sheds his inner trousers
at last. Hepaticas star the hills under leafless trees, the dogtooth violet hangs the damp valleys with golden bells.

The dinner of the month is dandelions. The small boy
digs them, going on all fours with his patches on his hind
quarters spread to the sun, stabbing them up with his silver
case knife. He brings home a pailful of green octopuses and
has to spend an hour washing the grit from them in the tub
by the well. His mother boils them two solid hours, with a
whole section of last year's pig salting and savoring them at
the heart of the old ringed iron kettle. The small boy eats
nearly a peck. The hired man is close second.

Anemones come out in the woods like drops of winter, and they tremble on the faintest breeze. The fish of the month is cod, the reach boat comes home from sea low with them, but the lobsters keep the man busy at each ebb of the tide. He goes from buoy to buoy, and the young son gets bitten deep by a crab.

The yellow of dandelions burns up like a light on the sky. The girls come home with baskets of wood violets. The young man goes now every evening in his boat to the island of the braids, and Grandma dreams of white and a wedding. The old mare brings a handsome colt, all legs, home from the pasture, and the small boy discovers, by holding a dandelion to her dimpled chin, that the molasses girl likes butter as much as he does. The columbine hangs her red, gold-lined bells on the cliff too high for the children to reach. The flowers come too fast to keep track of. The shadbush lights the firwoods up like snow, the rhodoras fill the evening swamp with purple smoke. Little boys throw their voices back in their throats and yodel, and other small boys, two farms and a bay away, hear them and answer their spring cry.

One night there is an explosion in all the trees, and people wake up in the morning to a world all new leaves. Goodbye, goose grease and camphor bags! The small boy flings off his shoes and runs barefoot to school. The bees swarm.

A swarm of bees in May
Is worth a load of hay.

The farmer puts on his veiled hat and takes his dip net down, but the bees get into his broad pants, between wind and water, and the little boy laughs to see his father leap out of them and run bare into the bay.

The baby sits up by himself. The mother puts salt pork on the big toe the small boy has run the rusty nail into. The winds are forever west. The rising sun turns whole forests into singing birds. Naked *Gemini* is the sign, and by Jeminy! the lambs are often twins in the pasture, and the small boy believes he will start off his family with twin boys, though how he will manage with two of himself at once is more than he knows. He brings the girl's books home in the strap with his own books, and he does the kissing that is done now, when they are by themselves and hunt for four-leaf clovers on the grass.

Now the plow point goes into earth, the spanned horses come up the fields trampling the bluets, and the plow shines like silver. The small boy walks the rolling furrows with joy arching his bare toes. His father lets him hold the handles of the plow for a round, and he goes with butts wide, bursting the stitches at his proud stern, and his mother will have much work to sew him together for school tomorrow. The lobster traps lie untended, and the crabs devour all the bait, for the farmer is all farmer for the moment and no fisherman. The potatoes are dropped. The big boy scatters the peas. The woodchuck plans a still larger nursery, seeing how near the peas will be to his domicile, and he goes down into his burrow to attend to the increase in his household. The crows congregate on the pines, they can hardly talk together for the water in their beaks as they watch the yellow kernels fall into the dunged hills. They laugh in scorn at the old pants and coat, with nothing but two crossed boards in them, masquerading as the farmer; they know he is much thicker through the pants than this. They go to bed hungry on purpose to stoke themselves with swollen sugared corn kernels to-morrow. The farmer comes in smelling of cow dressing and good dirt, and he sits tired in the kitchen by a gingerbread, in peace up to his crinkled eyes. Sweat is a sharp sauce to a good supper.

The light breeze blows the apple blossoms over the dark loam of the garden, for the land is white with apple trees now. Even the deep wild woods light up with pink fires of wild crab apples. A man walks through a honeycomb when he walks through a day, and the bees are a far-away thunder to the boy lying lazy, face down in the orchard grass. The swallows skim low, and it will rain in the night; and the old man is right, as they find by the clean puddles on the grass at sunrise. The crows are still empty and are in loud conclave in the pines, they cry over the fear they have that the twine string strung up last night over the garden rows is some kind of trap.

The wind veers south and blows the worm into the speckled trout's mouth, just as the adage said. The big boy comes home with a long string of speckled rainbows for supper. Rhubarb furnishes the year's first pies from the outside. The shotgun cracks the dawn, and a bold crow is hung with spread wings, head down, in the corn patch. The other crows gather for the funeral service on the pines, the widow screams the loudest.

School lets out for good, and the boys run the woods like a parcel of whooping red Indians. The lilacs wall the house round with white fires and purple.

The hired man comes home from his widow with his long moustaches drooping, and his big feet drag heavy on the ground. He has no appetite for a third piece of the vinegar pie next morning at breakfast, and he plays sad songs on his harmonica in the open-chamber half the night. He goes no more abroad. There is no more hard scrubbing behind his red ears, and the man is as little good about the farm as a last year's crow's-nest. Grandpa has much to say about the ways of widows, but the hired man chews his salt cod and says nothing. The big boy whistles "The Widow in a Cottage by the Sea," and the hired man goes off to the woodshed. The small boy finds him sitting low in his mind and his pants on the sawhorse.

The partridge drums all through a golden afternoon on an oak stump, and two proud, bright she-eyes drink in his bronze puffed ruff from among the tender young leaves. There are sky-blue eggs in the robin's nest, and three pearls in the grass thimble of the humming-bird, speckled eggs in the nest of the hermit thrush in the maple tree, and freckled eggs in the marsh grass where the sand-peep whistles. The small boy wades the brook with his overalls rolled high, and the molasses-candy girl sits on the bank and drinks in his clustered sunlit curls. Only the hired man is without love.

It is a wonder now to walk the woods. The leaves are still wrinkled and translucent, and they let the sunlight through. The columbine hangs the rocks with red horns and golden cups, and the bees are deep in them to their fuzzy tails. The seven-pointed star flowers float over the forest floor with only the shadow of a thread to hold them above the clustered leaves. From glossy leaves shaped like hearts the Canadian

Mayflowers go up like rockets and explode into snowy flowers too small to be believed. They sweeten the woods for miles. The purple bird-on-the-wing flies here fiercely in motionless flight. The bunchberry blooms spread out petals of ivory set on four leaves that are marked like globes with lines of longitude. The sarsaparilla sends up fountains of tripled leaves. The lady's-slipper opens her wide-grooved leaves, and up leaps a high stem, and a veined and swollen pink heart floats and beats all by itself on thin air. The speckled thrush hangs to a bough like a flower himself, and his throat swells out big with soft bells going higher and higher into loveliness.

It is May, new leaves and young blossoms, and the year is ready to burst at all seams.

COAST CALENDAR

★ ★ ★ ★ *June* ★ ★ ★ ★

COMES IN HIGH-RUN TIDES IN THE
bays and high tides of daisies. The fields are butter-and-egg
fields; buttercups fill all the swales, and daisies wash up the
hillside and spatter white on the sky. When the wind blows,
it is pure honey for air, and all bees come home heavy and
with their trousers dusted with gilt pollen. In the dawn, the
woodchuck eats all the young peas. The small yellow dog
digs furiously at the hole till only his hind legs are seen,
but the woodchuck whistles below and sasses the dog for
his trouble. Next dawn the woodchuck brings his wife and
all the neighbors, and they eat all the lettuce, too.

There are five yawning mouths for the robins to put
worms in over the side-porch door. The robins hop-skip
along the yard and pull up angleworms as long as themselves, tip down their heads, and listen for the next one
The small boy rows his own boat out to Goose Island and
back all by himself. He grows up an inch in the three
hours. The ovenbirds echo hollow through the leafy woods.
The qwoks cry hoarsely at their fishing all the livelong night.
Beans curve up through the garden, the halves of the resur-
rected old beans split, and the baby bean leaves come out.

A little boy and a small dog run for running's sake by the
hour, and then sleep in the warm sun curled so close together that it would take a good pair of eyes to tell which
is boy, which is dog.

Now is the season of lobster stew. The lady of the house
puts the children to work with hammers and breadboards,

and they crack the big claws and take the meat out whole. They suck the small claws and swallow that meat as their right. They save the white blood and the green tomalley. The bowl fills slow but sure. The mother puts the lobster meat on to cook in the lobsters' own juices. She puts in slabs of fresh butter, she pours in milk softly as the stew simmers on the slow fire, and she puts in cream. The family eat hot bowlfuls of heaven.

All the mornings are loud with crows, for the first batch of black babies is turned out now, and mother and father and all the neighbors scold and give advice and applaud as the young ones try their wings. The babies scream continuously for food, and their parents pour mussels and snails and kernels of stolen corn into the bottomless pits of their yellow throats. But the babies still bawl for more.

The hired man happens to be walking past a certain farm, and the widow calls to him through the kitchen window. He goes in with watery knees, feeling all pants and hands and big feet, the widow stuffs him full of oven-hot sugar cookies. Cookie after cookie goes in whole under the wide moustache, the man's eyes feed on the widow, and he loses all count of cookies and time and space. He comes home walking on pure air. He floats.

Grandpa goes on his tour of the orchard and declares the russets are poor but there will be many cherries. The cat gets the daring first-born of the robins, and a hawk takes the runt, but there are three young ones left as smart and as bright as any young robins in the world. The sand-peep leads out a file of brown fluff-balls on teetering legs thin as needles, and she shows the children what minnows are and how they are swallowed head-first, to save scratching the throat. Grandpa spots the lost swarm of bees in the hollow beech. The hired man gets a big hornets' nest for his widow's mantelpiece, but he gets punctured in three places on his seat and has to stand up during his evening call. The yellow dog goes courting five farms away but comes home with one ear ragged because of a collie ahead of him there.

Hives are filling up with honey. Buttercups and daisies, white clover, red clover pour sweetness into the combs. The hired man washes his ears till they glow like lanterns before he goes out every night. He even tries a bath in the toolshed, but he wedges himself in the washtub when he sits down in it, and it takes Grandpa and the big boy to get him free. He declares that even love is not worth such great trouble and goes back to his washbasin.

Barn swallows have clay houses hanging on every rafter, and the whole upper barn is full of beady, expectant eyes. The mother comes through the north window and drops her load into mouth number one spread open wide as a door, and off she goes for more. Father shoots in at the south and fills mouth number two, and away. Mother volleys in and feeds number three, and out. Father volleys home and stuffs number four. It is like clockwork, and never a miss or a mouth filled twice.

Grandpa tinkers with the clockwork in the kitchen Seth Thomas, and has two wheels at the end that he cannot find a place for. The clock never goes again. The cows eat wild onions, and the milk tastes strong at night. The crows grow tired of corn and shellfish and rob the yellow-hammer's nest in the dead popple tree of its eggs. The kingbird harries the black thieves into the thick woods. The little boy and the big boy hoe the kidney beans till their overalls stick to them. Then they jump out of their clothes and run into the waves and go under. The small yellow dog splashes with them in the sea. They go back to the hoeing crusted with salt.

Under the junipers in the pasture baby rabbits look at the world with their round new eyes. The small boy has not seen the one with the candy curls for weeks, but he dreams of her every night. The hired man saves up two dollars and buys the widow a ring with a stone that can almost cut glass. He is afraid to deliver it in person and bribes the small boy to take it to her in his name. The widow blushes deep and puts the ring away. She fills the empty boy up with spongecake till he is taut as a drum.

Never so many young ones as now. Young deer totter in the woods, young partridges scoot out of their eggs the instant they see the light, all the telephone wires are lined with baby swallows hung out to dry. There is a new boy in every reach boat, and all the old cradles are full again. The shores are laced with the shells of small horseshoe crabs that did not get on, and infant smelts, so transparent they are nothing but eyes, swarm in the sea. Every leaf is a nursery.

The young man goes in his new shoes and his putt-putt boat over the water, the family follow in the reach boat, dressed like a Sunday on a Thursday; and there is a wedding in the little white church at the island's tip where all the windows have waves in them. The young boy takes it all in, for he feels certain he will be next. The tall new wife starts housekeeping in the cottage on the cove, and burns her first johnnycake to a cinder.

The woodchucks turn now to the late peas. Winds are all west winds or south winds, and you would think the sea was a basket of kittens, the little waves run so gentle and soft. The best flowers now take to the woods. The lady's-slipper dangles by the purple bird-on-the-wing. The dandelions are suddenly little gray-haired ghosts. The corn is the length of a man's finger, and the dangling crow's bones show like snow in his feathers. Potato bugs appear.

The cuckoo warns it will turn hot, and the small boy hangs his tongue out at the hoeing. The girls play dolls in the shade. The bay turns suddenly alive at the dusk, and the tails of the shad smack the tide. Now the net is payed out of the reach boat by lantern light, cork line and lead line go over. The father and his sons sit quiet and drift with the stars. A cork bobs under the bow. Then the man stands and takes in a web of silver wires in the light of the lantern, and there is a great fish like a slab of the full moon choking to death in the mesh. Shad flop around the small boy's ankles till he is up to his knees in cold silver; he dozes, and wakes in his father's strong arms, being carried under the lantern-lit trees. Next day there is shad baked on the beech plank, and the boy fills himself up to his eyes. The grass at the cove is specked with flakes of pure pearl, and the small boy has miles of net to untangle of seaweed and to spread out to dry in the sun.

Grandma goes to town and comes home smelling of big, flat peppermints. The sign now is *Cancer,* the Crab, and the young boy has bushels of crabs to pound up for the quarreling hens. Grandpa shakes his head over the mares' tails in the sky. The vane wheels s'utheast, backs around no'theast, and it rains buckets three days. The first cinnamon roses burst open. The small dog runs afoul of a skunk and has to be buried in the garden to his nose. Tree toads laugh for the wet through the twilight.

The vane veers to the west, the clouds break, and the thrushes fill the moist world with sweet, sad, evening flutes.

Now milk tastes of white clover, the hives overflow with honey, the woodchuck's cup runs over, flowers star every inch of earth, and the fair-weather whitecaps flower the ocean.

> *And what is so rare as a day in June?*
> *Then, if ever, come perfect days.*

It is the warm month, the merry month, the marriage month, and tiptop high sun of the year.

COAST CALENDAR

★ ★ ★ ★ *July* ★ ★ ★ ★

COMES IN HIGH THUNDERHEADS. *Leo* is the sign, and he growls through the night; the panes light up from the quick glare of his eyes. Grandpa sleeps the thin sleep of an old man and mutters to himself in the dark about old haying days long ago. Haying is in the air. The smell of the red clover is heavy on the day after the shower. The lights on the daisies are going out.

The woodchuck brings his whole brood and lets them worship him for his good providing and sit munching in what he claims is his own patch of peas. But the house also has a mess of green peas for the Fourth. The braided strings of red firecrackers pop, the Roman candles hiss and cough out stars, and the small boy goes to bed with one good finger left on his right hand and crowded to the gunwales with tender peas and Kennebec salmon. Grandma dreams of red roses and knows the first baby down at the cottage on the cove will be a girl and very good-looking.

The feast of the month is wild strawberry cream. Wild strawberries hang the hayfields with dimpled rubies. It is now or never, before the haying. The girls stain their fingers with the berries, the small boy smells them out, going on all fours through sweetgrass and buttercups with his buttercup-colored dog beside him. He gets more in his belly than he gets in his pail. Baskets of strawberries come home. Mother hulls by the hour, and the girls all help, but the boy is making peapod canoes and cannot find the time, though he snatches some of the biggest berries from the dish. There is a ten-quart mountain of the berries at last. Mother gets her wooden pestle and crushes the berries into a red mash, grinding up even the seeds, for the deepest flavor is in those. She puts in ten quarts of sugar. She lifts the thick cream off her milk pans like folds of yellow velvet and stirs it all in with the berries. She shoos the boy off and puts the dish down-cellar. Next day, the wild strawberries are the dinner, in a ten-quart earthen dish, buttressed with cream-o'-tartar biscuits. The boy eats a quart of paradise.

Now the nights are millions of drifting sparks of fireflies, and the whippoorwill cries till he is a burden to hear. Wild briar roses set the world afire. The bees fill two golden tenement houses out of the white clover in the bay meadow. The thunder showers stand up white and lean over, growing like flowers as they come, the lightning plays on their petals, and the thunder comes long after the light. The small boy still half believes that thunder is big hogsheads being rolled down behind the sky, and when the rain comes, the staves in the hogsheads have burst and water gushes out. The sun goes out, it turns dark, it pours; but the sun comes out low, hailstones lie among the rose petals, and a rainbow spans the sea from one island to another.

They jump to the haying now, while the day is still deep in morning dew. Grandpa trims with his scythe by the house, the horses lean ahead hard, and the tall grasses fall parallel before the teeth of the clicking machine. Father sits on air, on nothing, beside his cutter bar, he shouts to his dark-sweating team. The dog noses out mice without hair or eyes, and the boy nurses them in the heat of his hand. The boats and the traps lie idle, for hay is making in the sun and more thunder in the air. The windrows run up over the hilly world. Each wind is sweet with them. The old man shows the young boy how to cock hay, combing the top straws into a roof; and the new wife learns how to make a custard pie from the old. The hands, smelling of hay, have shad for their dinner under the trees, and they joke about the many bones making it hard for them to pull the shirts off their backs at night. Loads of hay roll into the dark barn, with no wheels showing. The boy rides on a sweet peak of the Andes into the barn gloom. He treads the hay in a golden dusk and sneezes for the chaff. The big boy is lost in a new man pitching off the rack. The cows break into the kidney beans, but the yellow dog disperses them. Greenhead horseflies bring blood on the horses, the red spurts out where they have bitten. Men sweat, bare as Indians to the waist. Tempers grow short.

> *In winter there is room for rhyme,*
> *But it's short stories in haying time.*

Blueberries are bluing the pasture ledges. The girls go in deep sunbonnets after them, but the young boy wears a rhubarb leaf on his hair. The house smells of pies. Now a small boy picks potato bugs in the high great heat at five cents a quart, but there is cool lemonade at the row's end. The boy has almost forgotten what the molasses-haired girl looks like now, so long it has been since he's seen her. It is a fight to keep down the ragweed and pigweed in the garden. The hayers and hoers take a day off to go on the ocean, for the pollock are schooling. The small boy hooks a snowy fish the size of himself, they gaff it in, and the red streams from its sides and stains the bilge water. Wild raspberries come in the cut-down where the stovewood of two winters back came from. Mother lines the cellar with jams and preserves.

The hired man borrows the second-best horse, puts on his best pair of pants, and takes his widow to town on a Saturday night. But he breaks the headstall, has to lead the horse home, and pretty near wears his town shoes through. He gets his love home so late she is in a flurry as to what the neighbors will say, and doesn't take time to bid him good-night. The hired man crawls up to his chamber at two o'clock in the morning. Grandpa plagues him about the widow at breakfast, and the hired man loses his appetite at the fifth codfish ball and cannot finish his meal. Love thins a man down.

Blueberry-cake supper rolls around. Mother bakes five sheets of it, out of a vanilla dough into which she has stirred blueberries rolled in dry flour so they won't sink to the bottom. It comes out of the oven just in time for supper. The haymakers eat half a cake apiece, swabbing on knifefuls of new butter to lubricate it on the way down. The blueberries are all spattered through it, and it has no sogginess at the bottom. Father allows it is the best blueberry cake Mother ever made.

The roadsides are tall cornflowers the color of Grandpa's old blue eyes. Black-and-gold spiders in the marsh shake their webs out of sight, and the dragonfly goes into invisible death and hangs head down with his four new useless wings. Mullein candles are lit all up and down the pasture slopes, and their tall spikes of fire make a hot day feel hotter. Locusts fiddle wild. The sweet pink briar roses blossom right down the ledges into the sea. The young sand-peeps can fly short circles over the fair-weather waves. Bee-balm lifts its tower of blue hoods, and the wild vetch purples whole valleys. Wild morning glories open fluted cups, and their tendrils choke the little trees. The tame morning glories blue the early hours with unbelievable stars.

The heat is so great it can be seen quivering over the pasture. The mother partridge, with both wings hopelessly broken and dragging, cries pitifully and leads the yellow-haired small boy and his yellow dog a long ways in the woods. Then her wings heal, she goes up like thunder into the sky, and circles back to her chicks, calls them out of hiding, and goes on teaching them the way to scratch up grubs. The crows have full crops, and the children now fend for themselves. Young rabbits swarm. Foxes have full larders.

The cherry trees are loaded down with red, as Grandpa vowed they would be. The fruit hangs clustered on the sky. Mother runs up a host of pies and scalds out her preserve jars. But at sunrise next day she is wakened by piercing, drawn-out sweet notes of birds and wakes Father and the small boy. They run down in their night-tails. Sure enough, the trees are loaded with brown birds in black topknots, with beads set in velvet for eyes. They hang on the cherries and slice them to their stones. They flit from bough to bough making fire with their bright-hackled wings. They eat upside down. They pass the cherries along among themselves, from stained beak to stained beak. The man and the boy shout loud, but the birds stick to the fruit and will not be frightened away. Father runs for his shotgun. He lets the birds have it where they crowd thickest. The cedar waxwings rise then, in a golden cloud, whirr, and are gone into the blue sky. But the cherries hang in tatters, every spray bleeds. Mother can put away her jars. The small boy picks up a bird made of wind and sun, light and wonder. The bright thing bleeds red drops like small cherries in his hands. The boy is sorry.

The little dog pants with his tongue a good way out, but he gets up enough energy to run afoul of a raccoon and gets his ears bitten for his pains. The boy spends half of each day in the ocean, high-water time, learning to float on his back. His overalls are all that stand between him and the world, when he is out of water, and they have breathing holes at their seat. The last load of hay goes in, with a cluster of wild roses the farmer has put there upon it, as his father and his father's father did before him. Lobsters again are the harvest, once hay is in, though some of them are beginning to shed their shells.

It is the hay month, the fragrant month, hot month, month of the berries and sweat, month of white lightning.

COAST CALENDAR

★ ★ ★ *August* ★ ★ ★

COMES IN FOGS. LOST ATLANTIS comes unmoored on the Banks, sweeps in, and erases all land. The baby cries all night, but in the morning he has his first tooth. Boats pick their way between continents of fog, a sail comes out of nothing and towers close over the reach boat. Foghorns bellow through the nights; they wake the baby, he cries. The lobsters now are through with sprouting new shells at midsummer and are at the blush of new flavor; they are brought home by boatloads. Dogfish are dogging the cod, the fisherman pulls up a fish that is only a head. Sculpins alone come in whole, thorny and growling. But clams are a brisk commodity, and the young man makes enough on the flats to furnish his parlor. Grandma finishes a crazy quilt for the cottage.

This month's feast is an outdoors one, it is baked clams, Abenaki style. In the cove Father digs two bushels of long blue clams, and the boys fall to and gather mountains of driftwood and fresh rockweed. They make a quick series of fires, put rockweed on the coals, then clams, and cover all in with more seaweed. They sit, hungry, and smell the savor of hissing shellfish. On the edge of starvation they roll back the blankets of seaweed on the several fires, and boys, girls, women, babies, and men fall on the opened clams, tear them out, burn themselves to the bone, swallow the smoky tidbits whole, tears in their eyes, and all cry for more. One fire finished, they all move on to new uncovered ones, and they feast again. They eat the hot sun down the sky.

The flood tide puts out their embers near the high-water mark.

Salt hay is now in season, the men cut it with scythes and carry it on birch poles up out of the tide's way. The black flies sting the boy's eyes shut as he bends to turning the grindstone. They make the hay on the beaver dams, and a horse must have his sea legs on to pull the rack along the crest of the dams without sinking to his ears in the mire. Sandpeeps whiten the sky as they wheel by hundreds over the salt ponds. The small boy shoots his first shotgun. It is a muzzle-loader and longer than he is. He rams in five fingers of powder and shot, takes aim at the spoonbill, pulls the trigger. The earth comes up and hits him at the back of his head, and he sees many stars. But his brothers praise his shooting. And the spoonbill gasps and dies.

Horse-mackerel day, and the boy holds his breath far out at sea watching his father hold one end of a line with seven hundred pounds of mad fish on the other. A vast tail beats the boat's side, but the fish dies of a dart in the water and dyes the sea red. Blackberries load the pasture, but it takes a boy in iron pants to pick them. The boy walks barefoot to church, carrying the new shoes earned out of blackberries in his hand. He sits down by the road, puts them on, and goes squeaking and proud into church with no blemish on them.

The Indian god now puts on his tall feathers, the silk comes to the ear of the corn, and the cornsilk makes the small boy think of the hair on the girl he has not seen for so long. He steals over to her house, but the girl is gone visiting cousins. He hopes it is not boy cousins she has gone to see. He sits on the fence of her garden and aches all over under the hot evening star.

Sweet milk is swelling the ears of corn. The hired man swells out so with love he cannot sleep in his torrid chamber. He walks over to the widow's, but it is so late she has gone upstairs. The man sits on her fence with drooping moustache and watches her window long after her light is out. He aches till the star of morning. He is no good at the hoeing next day. Love leaves man in ruins.

String beans come in now. Grandpa picks a peck, and Grandma snaps them in her rocker as she works up a breeze on the side porch. There is a vast kettleful of beans for dinner, with a large continent of salt pork in their midst. There are new potatoes with the beans, the size of a boy's marbles, which Grandpa felt out of the hills with his long bony fingers. They are eaten skins and all, and are as tender as the beans they are cooked with. The hired man has five helpings of beans and wads them down with eleven of Mother's hot cream-o'-tartar biscuits. The cucumbers bristle with green spines up and down the garden. The lettuce is going by. The beets are thinned out for greens. The second crop of green peas comes in. The sunflowers line the garden's edge with staring golden eyes. The woodchuck has lost his shape.

Cornsilk turns brown, and the ears are the bigness of a farmer's wrist. The hired man picks five armfuls and rushes them to Grandpa and Grandma. They strip off the husks, and the small boy runs the yellow ears to the kettle his mother has boiling up and down on the stove. The dinner table groans with platters of steaming gold. There is hot johnnycake. They smear butter on the kernels and eat the corn as it melts. The cobs pile high at the little boy's place. But the hired man eats behind a range of the Andes. His vast moustache drips butter as the corn ear slides from east to west under it and comes out bare. Father slices the kernels off for Grandma, for she fears for her new teeth. The big boy pulls up even with the hired man, but the man speeds up by not using his knife and by letting his moustache butter the kernels, and he goes two ears ahead of the boy. He wins out, when the kettle goes empty, by one cob.

This night before the full of the moon, the hired man, full up to the eyes with the milk of the tasseled Indian god, does not bother to wash behind his ears. He marches his big boots over to the widow's place. He marches straight into the kitchen, takes the plump widow into his arms, and kisses her hard. The widow gasps, and the fat is in the fire. Fifteen minutes later, a bowed and tabby man climbs into the open-chamber by the ladder to his skylight, so nobody will see him, and goes to bed, pants and all. In the morning a strange, hard-faced man announces in a loud voice that widows are the poorest imitations of women there are, that he is through with them forever. Even Grandpa is taken aback and eats his oatmeal porridge without a word. The hired man sails into the garden and picks all the string beans, then all the peas. He says nothing at dinner, nothing at supper, and goes to bed with the swallows.

Now comes the fullest moon of the year, rising in the east as the sun stands in the west. The world is strange with two lights. The tide comes up so high it wets the Queen Anne's lace and the clovers. The great blue heron wades deep in silver.

It is the harvest moon. The combs are full, the crows are full, the partridges are pats of butter.

Grandpa teaches the boy where to look for the hazelnuts, two by two, in their prickly pods. Goldenrod sets the world on fire. Grandpa is sad to see it. One more year gone. The men split the hake and haddock and dry them in sun on the fish flakes. Eel skins are dried for the hinges to flails. The dog catches a woodchuck at last, but it is only an up-country cousin of John Henry's and won't be missed. New potatoes come from the garden. The boy sleeps little at night on account of the mercury leaves he has waded in bare feet. The baby cuts tooth number two, and there is rejoicing. Huckleberries pepper the islands, the children go in boats and pick them by crates; they earn their school shoes by the berries.

Now bays are goosefleshed by mackerel, and they take them by boat-loads, the nets groan with them. They salt them down by the barrel. The boy dreams of the chevroned tinker-mackerel, he tastes the fish in his dreaming.

Virgo's the sign. The boy sees Molasses-Curls in her father's boat, passing, and he loves her now more than ever. The boat is black with gold stripe, and longer and faster than Father's. She is the only child, and maybe the boat will come with her! He is promised a trip to the city, but fogs set in again. August means fogs, the *Old Farmer's Almanac* says so:

> *He knew how Roman legions looked, for he*
> *Had seen the Maine coast fogs march in from sea*
> *For many years now, in the August days.*

Winds are forever south, south, south.

All at once, wind falls. The arrow of the vane hangs still, then it leaps and points at the Pole. The north wind rises like a shout, trees turn white under it. That night the Dead Men dance, as Grandpa said they would, hand in hand, circle over circle, millions of them, faint and flickering, over the northern spruces. They make the night like day, and a boy holds in his breath to see these old ghosts of the Indians making holiday late at night. The grandfather sighs; the year's backbone is broken, it is goodbye summer. An old man has not so many summers left to him, and he is sorry to see one go.

It is the month of hoes and high weeds, a hazy month, and a tired one. But it fills the bins, it fills the barrels, it fills the jars and cellars, and men have much to thank it for.

COAST CALENDAR

★ ★ ★ *September* ★ ★ ★

COMES IN A MORNING ALL OPALS and turquoises and dewdrops strung like pearls on the Queen Anne's lace. The path the early fisherman takes to his boat shows dark in the watery grass. The crickets fiddle faster and faster in the dusty weeds, for they know their time grows short. There is a feeling of something about to happen, in the woods, on the water. But the days come in golden and blue, as though they would always last. The sign is the leveled *Scales*, and the year hangs at a delicate balance. Frostflowers follow the goldenrod, they star the ledges with mauve stars. The jay screams in the sumac.

Fried eels make a good dish for the time, for they take but little fire, and they taste their best at this season, the horseshoe crabs being in high flavor. The small boy provides a large family, cracking up the crabs, baiting his wicker traps with them, and stoppling the wood bottle up with the pine cover. He pulls up knots of them, holds them by the heads, smears himself with the gurry. But he skins them to a clean azure and runs to the house. Mother fries them, with chevrons slashed in their sides, in deep pork fat in the spider. It is the feast of eels.

One day, all at once, the birds flock up by hundreds, they wheel higher and higher, turn, and are gone for good to the sea and the South. Grandma starts her fall knitting and shoes the whole clan in the thickest of wool. The woods of a sudden fall quiet. Only the partridge sounds, beating a far-away drum, making far-away thunder. Now it is school once again. The bell rings loud at the window. Boys in unfamiliar shoes walk the deep dusty roads with good manners. Butter would not melt in their mouths. The little boy squeaks at his shoes, he walks with woebegone face. The small dog mourns on the headland, howling his heart out north, towards him. Fringed gentians unroll lace bluer than sky in the yellowed grass of the swales. The fisherman tars his seine, drags it glistening out of the kettle, and stretches it out black on the heads of the late red clover.

The small boy walks again with his girl. He entices her back of the stone wall and kisses her. She kisses back two for one. They go with their arms around each other, and their feet feel nothing but clouds. There comes a yell, a grinning boy hid in the alders has seen them. "Girl-boy!" he cries. The small boy puts down his *Arithmetic* in the ruts. He is calm as an adder. He hits the boy square on the nose. The other boy is a good head taller. The blood pours out of the taunter. They clinch, they roll in the road. The girl sees her love from the oddest angles. He is all breeches and bulges. He curves like an eel in his clothes, fights, and says nothing. They stand, they fall; the little boy now is under. But he gets to his feet and lets go with both fists. His belly shows through his torn blouse. The bigger boy breaks and runs for it. The small boy dusts off his seat. A tooth is gone in the middle of his smile. But it's a first one, there'll be another. The girl kisses him unabashed and helps him dust off his breeches. It is for life now. Both of them know it. The afterglow comes, the woods run pure gold, and the twilight is flutes of crickets. A small boy and small girl go home through a vast glory.

It is the month of marsh birds. Now sandpeeps come sweeping the salt meadows in myriads, turning silver as they wheel over the salt ponds. They spill down notes like bright beads as they turn, a hundred quick wings together. They dart along the ponds, tails up, bills down, teetering like dancers. High over the world in the tender gray sky of autumn, the four incredibly sweet flute sounds of yellow-leg plovers come silvery down. Then the long wings dip to the marsh grasses, and the birds alight on golden legs thin as clay-pipe stems. Slim tails nod, slim heads nod, their beaks needle the schools of minnows. They feed on silver, their slender silver bodies run with the wind along the beaded fringe of the tide, quick as thoughts, sharp as angels. And their flutes sweeten the afternoon with music so bright it is sad.

The small yellow dog is lonely as time. He goes with lonesome eyes and finds nothing to do. He drags out an old coat of the small boy and lies on it in the kitchen. The bees come home with honey of goldenrod close to earth for their heaviness. Bumblebees wallow in the last squash blossoms so heavy with pollen they cannot climb out at evening but must spend the night walled up in gold.

And on an evening all gold the hired man scrubs his ears till they shine and goes with slow steps over dying fields and makes up with the widow. She is very widowish and cool, she keeps her kitchen between them. But the man is willing to sit at a distance and feed on her starched apron and beauty. She fries doughnuts by the light of her reflector-lamp. The deep fat sizzles in her spider. It is a joy to the man to see her fork out the puffed circles and put them on the *Boston Transcript* to dry. Her heart softens a little at last, and she gives him the center out of a doughnut, fried to pure gold. She relents more and gives him a whole doughnut, the first one that is dry. Another. And another. The clock ticks on. The pile of doughnuts goes down, a man's heart goes up. The clock chimes ten. The widow comes to with a start. She says good-night. When she opens the door for him, she stands suddenly on tiptoe and kisses the hired man on his surprised moustache. The man staggers home, so full of wonder and love and doughnuts he can hardly put one foot before the other. But his moustache's long ends crackle with manhood, and he runs like a boy up the back stairs to his room and upsets two chairs in his abandon. Next day he tars two seines without stopping and leathers six oars. He comes home black as Egypt and lies down in his bed smelling of tar and peace.

All at once the woods become loud with the crows. They gather by armies in the pines, the sky is black with more coming. They scream and call in every key. One old crow sits on a dead oak and directs them. They form in lines on the limbs. They launch off by companies into the air, and new companies take their places. It is the gathering of the clans, and proud parents show off their offspring before the national congress. The president nods and clicks an approving beak.

The sky falls to the fields on every side now. The frostflowers cover every hillside over with sad bright blue. The single frostflowers stare with their single golden eyes, and the tall frostflowers stare with a hundred. Earth blossoms out with little suns bidding goodbye to the great sun wheeling lower and lower in the sky.

One sudden day a maple stands in flames, and there is white on the north side of all things. The crickets are hushed for good. Next morning the frost is white over all the fields.

Now it is smelts, at the ebb low and flood low they net them. The older man stands at the dory's stern and pays out the seine, corks one way, leads the other; the younger man rows with braced feet; they cut off the flow of the channel. They leave the net quiet, it loops with the tide. They loosen one end from its stake and row fast across to the other. They draw the loop smaller and smaller; it comes in a boatful of silver. The small boy dances for joy in dancing bluefish, in herring, in capelins, in smelts, up to his crotch. There are eels, and he catches a pipefish. By daylight, by lantern light, and by moonlight, they sort the fish over on the wharf. Big smelts in one box, small in the other. There is every kind of fish hissing in the spider up at the house. The men cart their fish to the town and the train for Boston and brains.

The boy makes torches of the cattails by dipping them in kerosene; he lights up the night and burns four holes in his breeches. The baby goes into a standing stool his father has made. Grandpa looks at the squirrel's fur, after the big boy has stripped it off; it is thick, it will be a hard winter. The small boy finds fractions hard, but geography is right up his alley. He has barked his shins on it on this coast.

A night comes when the house shakes, a gale blows the elm trees double. It is here. The farmer knows it even in his sleep, and groans. The small boy wakes up and wonders at it. There is great sorrow in the air, all the birds and the wide world grieve. It is the sun crossing the far-off equator:

Three things there are which never fail:
Taxes, death, and the Line Gale.

It is the end of green and growing. In the morning the air is snowed with all the maple leaves of the world, they fly away like sparks of red and yellow fire.

Now the catch is herring. The reach boat goes far up the hill of the Atlantic and comes home down to the water's edge with the slim fish. Now the boy must lug popple wood to the smokehouse and blow up the coals to make smoke till his eyes are as red as the herrings'.

It is the month of turning corners on time and all things. Yet the month means a full smokehouse, a full cellar, and a fat belly.

COAST CALENDAR

✶ ✶ ✶ *October* ✶ ✶ ✶

COMES IN FRESH GALES AND LEAVES miles high in the sky. All the leaf trees have caught afire now, and the red and golden flames of them fill the woods with vast light. Grandpa can read his newspaper without his spectacles by the July sunlight coming out of an October tree as he sits under the boughs at twilight. The air runs wine, the earth runs amber cider, and the sea is a fairyland of whitecaps. Surf booms on the reefs, and Easter lilies stand up at the ocean's edge. The days are like the insides of Sandwich-glass plates, and all beaded with light.

Now apples drum the world, and the small son shakes down a heavy rain on the big son's back and Grandfather's bald head. He gets his breeches smacked on their blind side for his trouble. The big boy catches the small one bending and stings him hot on his seat with a nodhead.

The apple now has its day in the kitchen, and the month's feast is the deep pork apple pie. Mother peels the Northern Spies and covers the floor with fragrant S's and C's and O's. She pares the white fruit and gets out her deepest iron skillet. First a cushion of piecrust, then a layer of apples, a lacing of fat salt pork in strips, then apples, then pork, then apples. She sprinkles on brown sugar and cinnamon thick, dashes in a splash of molasses from the old flowered jug, and laces all with quick strings of honey. She claps on the thick top crust, notches a flock of flying geese across it, and sprinkles on cold water, to make it flaky. She claps the pie into a hot oven. Apple juice, pork fat, honey, sugar, and cinnamon fuse. Mother takes out one of the Delectable Mountains, sets it before the menfolks at table, and they carve deep in glory!

The sign is *Scorpio*, the Secrets. The small boy broods over the picture and the place the arrow points to on the Naked Man in the *Old Farmer's Almanac;* he closes the book and feels guilty when his grandsire comes into the kitchen to read about the coming weather. But *Scorpio*, too, on this coast, is the big-clawed lobster. He sculls the bay at his tastiest now, he comes home by hundreds in the reach boat, with his dangerous jaws made fast with wedges of white pine. The fisherman moves his hand among living shears, he picks the lobster up with finger and thumb and just back of his stickpin eyes. The big boy handles the reach boat as well as his father.

Now nights are full of shooting stars. The northern lights burn below the Great Dipper. Never so many stars as now; they dust the heavens deep from the north to the south. The baby cuts his third tooth. Grandma dreams of a friend, dust these fifty years in the graveyard. There will be news. The father leaves clamming and opens the land with his clam hoe; the potatoes dot the furrows for miles, and a small boy has a cricked back from so much bending and picking up the big ones. The farmer brings his dory home filled with apples to the gunwales, and the boy sits on the top of them and sings. The cider press pours out a dark silk cloth of running honey.

The hired man carries a whole sack of the best apples when he goes for his tryst at his widow's, and he brings a part of the sack back within him, for he gets outside of a whole apple pie—save for one piece that falls to the widow—by the time he comes back at the crow of the first rooster of morning. He washes his ears and combs out his moustache every other night now, and the widow's lamp burns beyond midnight. But the hired man's work does not suffer next day. He does the work of three young men. He goes down the potato patch with wide legs, making the potatoes fly, and it takes a smart small boy to keep the new patches on his old pants in sight in the row as he rolls out potatoes. He runs to the house with a whole bag on his back and turns the cellar to thunder with the potatoes he pours down the spout. He runs back to his hoe and scolds the boy for not picking up faster. He pulls all the kidney beans in an afternoon, and Grandpa has three whole days of stacking the beans before him. Between them, the small boy sweats blood trying to keep up and shake the earth from the bean roots. The beans rise high as a man between the white birch stakes.

The yellow dog digs for woodchucks on the edge of the garden. Yellow pumpkins and squashes appear everywhere, now the potatoes and bean vines are torn up. The hired man piles up a pyramid of hot suns at the garden's center. A pumpkin that a boy cannot get from the ground, that is twice the size he is through the butts, the man balances on one wide palm as though it were an apple. For the tide of love runs high and smooth, and nothing can stand before him. He pulls all the beets in an hour.

The rabbits are taking to the swamp where the grass is still green and tender. The crows are falling quiet and are taking to the deeper woods. Grandpa is hugging the stove closer mornings. For there is an edge on the air, and the frost is white on all hills at sunup. The last golden eyes of the frostflowers close even in the shelter of the briars. The rose-apples begin to shine everywhere, now the rose leaves are withering. The white alder puts on her berries for Christmas.

On the marsh the ivory cranberries blush deep red on both cheeks because of the heavy frost-fall. The small boy goes deep into the bog in his rubber boots to get the largest and best of the berries. Mother and the girls bring them home by the basketful, and Grandma puts them into the tub of water to pick out the floaters. The fattening geese will have a good sauce to go with their meat. The small boy mashes up the small turnips that are boiled in the outdoors kettle, and the geese eat till their crops make them one-sided.

Bees make no sound now on the meadows. The earth smells of frost of a morning and of dying leaves of a night. The smoke of great burning lingers through all the afternoons. The little dog comes home early to his place under the warm cookstove. But the hired man minds no cold, he goes with his moustache full of frost to mind his widow. His feet are white with hoarfrost when he comes home hot under the stars of morning. For he carries his love like a whole cookstove with him.

When the vast sun rolls behind the spruces, the cock partridge swells on his lichened stump with a ruff of burnished bronze. He bathes in the dying fire of the sun, his feathers run with their own fire. His eyes gleam like sparks. He will take the sun's place, he vows, and his speckled fat spouse and their offspring believe him. Then a twig snaps, the cock's ruff falls, he grows slim as a serpent. All the partridges freeze, and they hear the stealthy steps coming. Then the fox that goes on his hind legs and carries the lightning in a black bough comes in sight, and a stand-ing small fox and a tame yellow fox behind him. The cock turns to thunder, roars into the sky, keeping a birch between him and the hunter. The lightning stabs, but he whirls away safe. Then the hen goes up in her thunder, but the lightning stick is double, fire blazes red, and she falls in blood and torn feathers. And the sun goes into the earth.

Ducks fill the bays. The farmer gets up at the crack of day, his shotgun booms from the blind he and the boys have built, and the winged coot falls plumb to the water. The small boy's eyes are like two holes burned in a blanket with his being up most of the night, but he loves it. His father lets him shoot the twelve-gauge, the sheldrake takes off in a great squawking. The boy is proud of his black-and-blue shoulder. The big boy has three black ducks for his day's work. Mother picks pinfeathers out with tweezers; there are new feathers for her featherbed.

Brush fires gleam. The nuts are falling for the frost. The small boy comes home twice his regular size through his breeches. The butternuts take hours to get out whole, but the beechnuts come out easy from their triangles of brown. The beans are stacked for the threshing. The popcorn is hung up braided by its husks for a winter's feasting.

> *Water's frozen in the pail,*
> *Heap the corncrib, swing the flail!*

The fall plowing opens the land to the healing of frost, the days grow solemn still, smoke stands straight up to heaven. Little pools wrinkle with thin ice of a morning.

The small boy sets his traps now, and he reeks of skunk when he sits by the hot stove at school. The teacher sends the boys out to drive the skunk away from the schoolhouse. The bees fall quiet in the hive. The boy carries a pumpkin almost as large as he is through the hazel dusk, he puts a head all fiery eyes at the window of the Molasses Girl. She shrieks, but she comes out smiling and takes the boy in to a loaf of spiced gingerbread. Little ghosts in short pants and Mother's sheets troop the spruces with jack-o'-lanterns grinning with triangular teeth and square eyes. The old man shivers in his lean coat, for more than the cold. He comes bringing home the last ear of corn the gleaners missed in the gloaming.

It is October, and the harvest housed and home.

COAST CALENDAR

★ ★ ★ *November* ★ ★ ★

BEGINS WITH LOW CLOUDS, AND IT seems the clouds stretch off to forever. Grandma sees a winding sheet in her evening candle, and is troubled. The sea mourns the night through. The small boy is glad for the desk by the stove at school. He lies and sees pictures of Arthur and his Knights in the coals when his father boils a pot of lobsters by night at the shore, and the clouds of sparks from the spruce are doubled by the dark water. It grows colder and colder. The ocean is troubled at the high sky-line; far islands are uneasy and lift in mirages, leaving the sea and having only a stem to hold them to water. It comes off soft and rains. It comes off cold and freezes. But the pools the boy hoped to slide on have only air under them in the morning. The earth is strangely still.

It grows dark at midday, a snowflake zigzags down, and another. The first snow flurry ices the grass. But earth is blown bare by an hour of wind. The man goes with his axe to the sprucewoods, he cuts brush, and he and the children bank the house with evergreen laces up to the clapboards, as the Indians banked their houses before them. The girls gather hemlock cones to gild. The little dog sticks close to the kitchen stove. Grandpa keeps him company. The wind off the sea grieves at the house's eaves.

Sagittarius is the sign, the Bowman, and the long arrows of the southbound geese go over. The old man sees them and is sad, remembering bygone springs and falls. The sign is the *Centaur,* the half-horse, half-man; and the coast man is

like him and double; one foot on land, one in the sea. He brings home smelts in his cart, his corn in his clam-rocker. He plows the fall fields, and he furrows the dark bay by boat. He milks the tame cow but has his hand in wild mackerel. He pulls the rutabagas today but pulls in green lobsters tomorrow. He is tiller but carpenter, too, and he keeps his boat's engine running. He is his busiest now under his *Centaur* sign. He takes in his traps for winter, hangs his nets up in the fishhouse, cuts the stovewood, breaks in the steers, hawks his clams and eggs in the village. He has more work than he can shake a stick at.

The day the small boy loves comes in raw. The pig is stuck in the pen, his thinning squeals go up to the welkin. Then he hangs pink as a cherub in the shed over a tub, free of his bristles. He is laid open like a canoe, his ribs braced apart with oak stretchers. There is hog's haslet for supper. Next day the centaur goes into the firs with his rifle along his thigh. The little boy is one pace in back, his twenty-two imitating his father's rifle. Deep in the firs is an orchard, where once a house stood, and they creep towards the gnarled and ancient trees. A white flag goes up, waves this way and that, but the rifle stabs fire, the flag falls and lies still. The boy runs and kneels, and he watches the light go out in wide eyes on the frozen ground. He is sad for a bit. But the buck is a four-pronger. The man carries the deer home over his broad shoulders. That night it is venison blanketed hot in singed bacon. The buck hangs by his heels in the shed, next to the pig, for the winter.

Cut off the ears, dig out the pig's eyes. Put ears and the pig's head into the iron kettle. Boil in salted water till the meat falls from the bone. Run the meat through the chopping-tray. Add sage and chopped raw onion. Add the stock to the meat, sprinkle in bay leaves and marjoram, set away in the low crock to cool. Slice, as you would cake, this jelly of the gods. This is the feast of hog's-head cheese!

Father misses his annual tidbit, the pig's tail. He demands it at supper. No one knows a thing about it. But the hired man's moustache droops to his plate, his eyes droop, he says nothing. And a mile away a plump widow is sitting down to the roasted curl of a pig's extremity, polishing her knife on her napkin, with lovelight in her eyes.

The crows press their breastbones on the leafless boughs at night, but they flap off with ragged wings and gaunt crops to the ebb in the morning and look for mussels to carry to the pasture ledges and break open for breakfast. The bees sit comfortable in their dark house with the light of summer warming them from their honeycombs. But the partridges run mad in the dark of the moon and fly blindly away to the four winds. It is the month of broken families.

The little Molasses-Candy Girl comes to supper at the house of the little boy with curly white-pine shavings on his head. There is a sea-moss-farina pudding in her honor, and the girls of the house make her laugh with bright talk of dolls' dresses. Molasses Candy is the center of the meal. But the little boy has lost his tongue, and he keeps his eyes on his pudding, so shy he is at having his wife-to-be for the first time at his table. The big boy talks for him, and his father gives the house a good name by helping the girl to a second plate of the pudding from the deep sea. Everybody is on his Sunday behavior. The hired man is all graces and shows off his best table manners, crooking his little finger out handsomely as he navigates his teacup to his moustache and back. He basks in the thought of how the next guest may be a widow about to become a wife and how he will shine before her. The little boy finds his lost tongue only when he is seeing the girl home under the low November stars. It is cold, but the boy comes home warm because he has kissed the girl at her door and carries the radiance with him on the dark road. Love is better than a fire of beechwood.

The rabbits are turning white in the swamp where the bushes are dusted each morning with hoarfrost. They run and leap with no fear of a yellow dog now. For he hangs to the house and hugs the fire. John Henry Woodchuck is beginning to get sleepy as the juicy grass roots wither. John Henry is digging his burrow deeper and deeper below the level of the frost. The sun is lower in the sky each day, and all good things must come to an end. John Henry knows it, and he blinks his drowsy eyes. It is the coming of the long sleep.

And the hired man comes reeling home on a bleak and overcast day. His moustache hangs at the ends like a flower after a frost, and in his woebegone eyes the sun has set for this year. He speaks to no soul in the house. He goes up to his chamber under the eaves, gets out his mouth-harp, and plays "Bingen on the Rhine" over and over late into the night. Grandpa knows, all the house knows, and all the house keeps quiet. It is the widow. Next morning Father brings home the melancholy news. The widow has sold out and gone to California to live with her brother. Widows, like all good things, come to an end.

A slim new moon, whetstoned by frost, hangs tangled in the thorns of the leafless briar bush. There is nothing young in the world now to wax as its horns wax—not a bud, not a nestling, not a snake or mole, not a love for a widow even. The moon wastes its silver on dead thorns. The lonely last woodcock, with wide eyes full of fear of death at the nose of a dog, crouches his last northern night with the moon in the briar.

Now hams go to the smokehouse, and the bacon strips are hung in the chimney. Nights are festooned with sausages, and sage is the seasoning of the month. The boy grows taut as a drum. The gulls have come inshore, and they cry always, lonesome and hungry. Slush ice is making at the bay's edge. The baby upsets his high-chair.

The day of days comes, the reach boat is pulled out of the tide. The horses pant, and the white wonder comes up on its cradle. It is roofed in under the pines. The bees, deep in the hive, start their glassy wings going to keep their hearts alive. All the dories are overturned under the trees. It spits snow from the north. It comes off a hard freeze, the ponds in the swamp are solid. The small boy learns to skate, and he dusts all the snow off the ice with his breeches before he masters the secret. But the big boy grinds-bark backwards, showing off to his sisters. Next day the small boy falls only twice and learns how to stop when he wants to.

And the holy Thursday comes at last, and a whopping turkey, a dozen squash pies, two dozen mince, and a hundred tarts trembling at their open hearts with crab-apple jelly. It snows uncles and aunts. It rains cousins. There are hazelnuts, apples red, green, and golden, beechnuts, and cranberry sauce molded into stars. There is joy in the air, and whiff from the oven is Eden.

Hurrah for the fun! Is the pudding done?
Hurrah for the pumpkin pie!

When the smoke clears away from the long table, and the uncles are gone into the future filled men, Grandpa looks at the turkey's naked breastbone. It is all white. The snow will lie deep this winter. That is best, for "Open winters mean fat graveyards." The snow will lie deep.

And in the morning, Grandma weeps, and Grandpa lies still on his bed. He will not eat that last ear of corn he saved, nor wade the deep snow coming. The gulls mourn over the bay.

It is November, month of farewells. The men and the boats go home.

COAST CALENDAR

★ ★ ★ *December* ★ ★ ★

COMES IN SNOW FLURRIES AND biting blows. The new mound in the graveyard is covered over deep, as Grandpa's turkey bones said it should be. The white border of the bay grows each day wider, and the ocean narrows and turns a black-blue. The farmer roasts skates' fins, and tells the boys about his war while the wind howls outside. All winds are north or northwest. All winds have snow in them. But the year's yield is housed home safe. The girls sew dolls' dresses. The days draw in, and the hens scratch for the hot corns in the straw in the henhouse in a four-o'clock dusk. A thieving mouse, put to sleep by sluggish bee-stings, is being walled up neat in wax in the silent hive.

The boy finds the evenings a burden, after school, and he makes a gilt dust as he bends to the bucksaw by lantern light. Grandma grieves in her Boston rocker. The cows chew their cuds side to side through the short day and the long night and have no complaint. The big boy milks ten cows and squirts a long squirt of white on the small boy's ears where he sits with them wide and milks his one Jersey. The small boy squirts back, but misses.

It snows all day and night, in the morning the pine trees droop to the stone wall under the weight of white furs. The woodchuck puts out the light and goes to bed for this year. Goodbye, John Henry! And sweet dreams of young peas! The winds skip over the bays, butting the islands with their furry heads. The house is alive with secrets. The girls hide packages done up in red strings in the bureau. The boy is making a toy sled for his Candy-Curls and dulls his father's best gouge. The nets hang like cobwebs in the silent fishhouse. A thousand herrings with open mouths and wide eyes hang parallel on the sticks in the smoke-house. The hams in the chimney are mahogany brown. The small boy goes belly-bunt down the hill and half a mile out on the bay ice.

It is now *Capricorn*, the Goat, and the boy butts his way through the powdery trees to school and butts the boys in the snow fort with lowered head for all the flying snowballs. The big reach boat is only a mound of snow at the cove. The upper bays are highways now, and huge horses smoke at their nostrils as they draw the piled beechwood over the water. The children go one after one over the ocean to school, keeping far apart, in case one goes through. There are black rifts of water by the shore where the tide rises and falls, and the children must jump them. But danger is a good sauce to a day.

School lets out with a burst of carols, and the small girls go home clutching the red net bags of striped candy. The rabbits leave three-cusped tracks by the alders, and there is a large dent where one has sat down to philosophize on the quiet white world. There are speckled feathers where the owl has made his dinner. The boy comes shouting home on his father's broad shoulders for the last time in his life and sees his homelight from a higher place than he will ever see it even as a man. It is farewell to small-boyhood.

Now it is hard on Christmas. Uncles come over the bays without boats, with icicles on their grizzled moustaches and a pocketful of sea-soned pine to whittle into fine boats for a young boy. Aunts gather and talk of steamed puddings and hooked-rug patterns; one works a hen that is so wooden she must lay Connecticut nutmegs. The biggest gan-der is shut up in a small pen, and he wonders at the mess of sweet turnips he is fed five times a day. The girls go for ground pine and running evergreen. But the small boy is trusted with the best axe and goes to bring in the fir tree. His breath is blue and big around him. It is his first Christmas tree. Last year big brother got it. Now he has inherited the honor. He finds the right tree by a ledge in the pasture. He walks around it three times, to make sure it is full on all sides, the north as well as the south. He fells it, he shoulders it and covers his coat with pitch; he comes home stumbling in the drifts, under the single first star, deep in the tree and Christmas to his eyes and heart. The tree is set in a box. Popcorn strings festoon it. The girls do the indoor trimming. The presents go on slyly. The uncles drink the hard cider deep into the night and talk of the hardness of aunts.

The small boy has hard work to sleep, he counts the rooster's crows, the stars slide over slow. But the window grows a little gray at the third cockcrow. He gets one stocking on inside out, forgets the latches to his breeches, tumbles downstairs, and opens the long package with his name. It is what he has ached for: a twenty-two rifle, longer and better than the one descended to him from big brother! He sits on the peak of his life, from now on it will be all downhill. He wraps the gun up and steals back up to dreams of bringing down a buck in the balsams. The girls shout through the house from the morning star till breakfast. It is flapjacks and maple syrup, hulled corn and molasses. The girls all have sleds, and the boy breaks them in for them on the orchard hill. The gander comes smoking in his fat, Father saves the boy the outside piece with the crackling skin. It is steamed apple pudding cut with a string, and more cider for all the uncles. Grandma in her Boston rocker reads the chapter in Matthew in the old family Bible. The melodeon is warmed up. The boy on all fours helps pump the pedals with both hands. Aunts who sing only once a year let themselves out. The shrill children's voices quaver.

> Shepherds sat upon the ground,
> Fleecy flocks were scattered round,
> And the brightness filled the sky,
> And the angels sang for joy
> On that Christmas morning!

A sleepy small boy, stuffed with popcorn, leans in the firelight on his father's knee. He thinks of molasses-candy hair, the stars twinkle at the frosty windows, the night wind blows, the firelight makes shadows dance huge over the ceiling. The boy hugs his gun and dog to him; he goes down the steep hill of sleep.

The Arctic owl comes back from the north, scaling home into the spruces on the white wings of a snowsquall. He finds his old seat on the popple stump, which fits his contours so well, and he looks over the young rabbits to pick out his supper. Winter is here for keeps. The field mice extend their tunnels under the snow, the barn mice gnaw new doorways in the grain bin, and the house mice creep to the cheese by a new street. The bees creep to a new comb in the hive. The crows hug their spiny roosts and have nothing to creep to at all.

The hired man grows restless nights. His love-sorrow has healed now, and he burns to try out his Christmas socks in the drifts. His big tracks make wider and wider circles each night around the farm. He is looking for a farmhouse where there are no tracks of a man on the snow.

The small boy goes into the firs to try out his new rifle. The yellow dog finds so many fresh tracks he cannot decide which rabbit to run and fills the woods with yelps. A squirrel laughs at the dog from a high limb, but his laughter is cut short, and there will be squirrel soup for supper. The new rifle has its first notch! The boy dangles with five squirrel tails when he stops in at the Molasses-Candy Girl's house on his way home to look over her presents and her. He promises her the best of his skins for a doll's coat. He walks home feeling big and toeing out like a man.

And the hired man finds his widow. She is nine farms away, she is not so plump as the other one, she has a mole on her left cheek, her house is not so large, and she has three boys full of the Old Harry. But a widow is a widow. And the boys can be broken into use at the bucksaw. They need a father's hand on their pert untamed breeches. So the wash-basin comes into use again, and the comb goes through a moustache that crackles with electricity and love. The year is not a total loss after all.

Out in the maple grove the snow buntings have arrived from the Arctic. They glitter like sparks. Their heads tip sidewise, their tails stand up saucy. The rabbits romp and roll and kiss noses in the snow.

Now the days come shining, the days come snowing. The old calendar goes into the stove, and the new is hung up back of the woodbox. The new almanac is hung by the mantel. The baby stands alone, teetering, for the first time. He has joined the upright animals for good. He crows and falls on his face. But he knows now where he belongs, and he will be up there again.

So the year draws to its end. The man casts up his accounts. Life reckons up the old and turns to the new. A life gone out, but a life come in. A new boat and a new boy. The dories safe in the cove. The smokehouse full. The cows under cover. The mows nearly up to the eaves still. A boy old enough to run with a girl. A smart wife. A son safely married, a grandchild in the offing. And the farmer still trotting a baby on his knee! A good year, and so it goes out. And God be on this saltwater farm! *Amen!*